BASEBALL'S GREATEST
MYTHS AND LEGENDS

by Elliott Smith

CAPSTONE PRESS
a capstone imprint

Published by Capstone Press, an imprint of Capstone
1710 Roe Crest Drive, North Mankato, Minnesota 56003
capstonepub.com

Library of Congress Cataloging-in-Publication Data
Names: Smith, Elliott, 1976- author.
Title: Baseball's greatest myths and legends / Elliott Smith.
Description: North Mankato, Minnesota : Capstone Press, [2023] |
   Series: Baseball's greatest myths and legends | Includes bibliographical references
   and index. | Audience: Ages 9-11 | Audience: Grades 4-6
Summary: "Did a major-league pitcher really hit a bird with a fastball in the middle of a
   game? What did a goat have to do with the Chicago Cubs not winning a championship
   for more than 70 years? Did Babe Ruth really point toward center field just before hitting a
   big home run in the 1932 World Series? Prepare to uncover the real stories behind these
   and other great baseball myths and legends!"-- Provided by publisher.
Identifiers: LCCN 2022025141 (print) | LCCN 2022025142 (ebook) |
   ISBN 9781669003458 (hardcover) | ISBN 9781669040217 (paperback) |
   ISBN 9781669003410 (pdf) | ISBN 9781669003434 (kindle edition)
Subjects: LCSH: Baseball—Miscellanea—Juvenile literature. | Baseball—History—
   Juvenile literature. | Legends—Juvenile literature.
Classification: LCC GV867.5 .S65 2023 (print) | LCC GV867.5 (ebook) | DDC 796.357—dc23
LC record available at https://lccn.loc.gov/2022025141
LC ebook record available at https://lccn.loc.gov/2022025142

Editorial Credits
Aaron Sautter, editor; Bobbie Nuytten, designer; Donna Metcalf, media researcher;
Polly Fisher, production specialist

Image Credits
Alamy: ZUMA Press Inc, 25; Associated Press: AP Photo, 27, Jose Campos/VWPics, 26, Ted S. Warren, 14; Getty Images: B Bennett, 11, Bettmann, 7, Historical, 19, Michael Reaves, 24, Norm Hall, 5, Ron Vesely, 29, Sports Studio Photos, 9, TASOS KATOPODIS, 28, The Stanley Weston Archive, left cover, Transcendental Graphics, 10, 17, 20; Library of Congress, 6; Shutterstock: Harold Stiver, right cover, 15, Hrytskevich, (frame) 19, Michael Rayback, (baseball) design element, Milos Kontic, (players) design element, Nick N A, (frame) 20, Robert Adrian Hillman, (ink splat) design element; Sports Illustrated: Bob Martin, 21, John W. McDonough, 13, Robert Beck, 23

Table of Contents

Words in **bold** are in the glossary.

Tied Up

In baseball, there are many close plays. Many happen at first base. Think of when a runner and the ball get to first at the same time. Some think the tie goes to the runner. Is this true? No. It's a **myth**. It's the **umpire's** choice. Safe or out!

Baseball has many myths and legends. Let's explore some of the biggest.

Legendary Called Shot

A major legend happened at the 1932 World Series. The New York Yankees played the Chicago Cubs. Babe Ruth was a Yankees star. He was a legendary home run hitter.

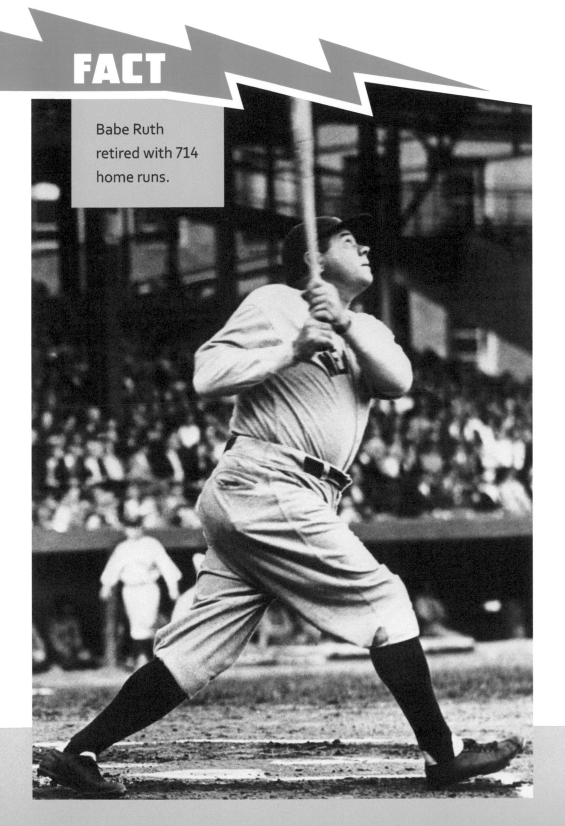

Babe Ruth retired with 714 home runs.

But Ruth's most famous homer is a mystery. Fans love to talk about it. Did Ruth **predict** hitting a home run in the World Series? No one knows. Even Ruth never said.

1932 New York Yankees

Babe Ruth

In the fifth **inning**, Ruth pointed at something. Was it the booing fans? Or was he calling his shot? Photos of the event are unclear.

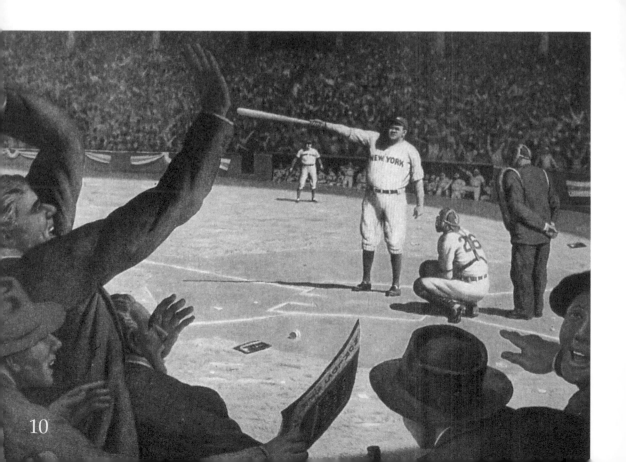

Ruth took two strikes. Then, SMACK!
He smashed a huge homer over center
field. It's still one of baseball's most
legendary plays.

A Doomed Bird

Randy Johnson is a Hall of Fame pitcher. In 2001, he played for the Arizona Diamondbacks. Johnson will never forget one game that year. He threw a powerful fastball. But then something happened.

A bird flew across the **infield**. The ball hit the bird. Poof! Feathers flew everywhere! The stadium staff quickly cleaned up the mess.

The pitch didn't count. But Johnson was upset about the bird. He wouldn't talk about the event for years. The moment is still part of baseball **lore**.

FACT

Randy Johnson led Arizona to win the 2001 World Series. He was elected to the Baseball Hall of Fame in 2015.

Who Invented Baseball?

Many people think Abner Doubleday invented baseball. That's not true. He did grow up in Cooperstown, New York. The Baseball Hall of Fame is located there. But Doubleday didn't create the game.

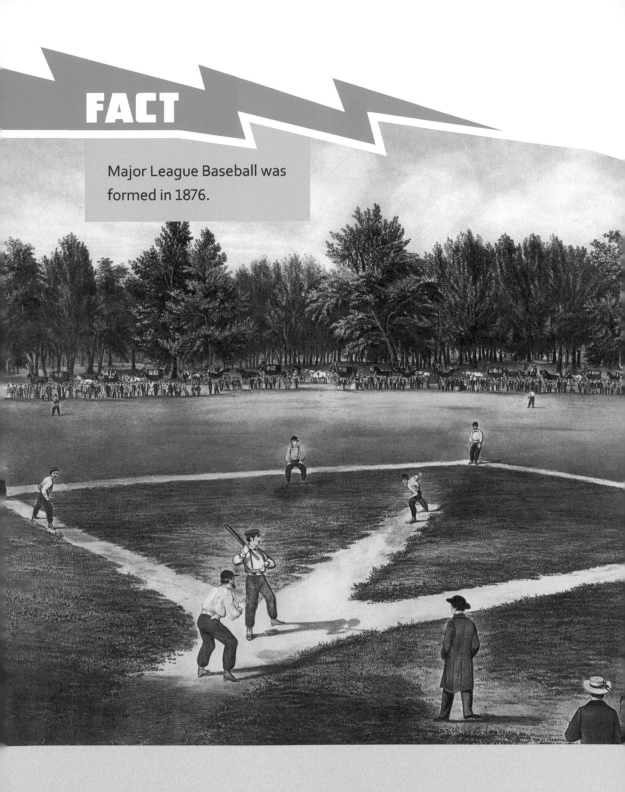

Major League Baseball was formed in 1876.

In 1907, some fans researched baseball history. Abner Graves said that Doubleday invented the sport. But Doubleday was a soldier and writer. He had no experience with baseball. Yet everyone believed Graves' story.

Abner
Doubleday

Some say Alexander Cartwright Jr. created baseball. He made some rules that are still used today.

Cricket and rounders are like baseball. The games may have **influenced** the sport. Nobody is sure if baseball was created by one person.

Alexander Cartwright Jr.

Cricket players in Pakistan

Highway Homer

Phillies player Bryce Harper is one of baseball's best hitters. The outfielder's power is exciting.

A legend grew after he hit a home run in 2020. Some people think the ball flew over the stadium wall and hit the highway. Talk about power!

But don't believe this tale. Harper's homer did go far. And a highway does run behind the Phillies' spring training stadium. But the road is more than 600 feet (183 meters) from home plate. It would have been cool. But Harper's big hit didn't reach the highway.

Philadelphia Phillies' spring training ballfield in Florida

FACT

Bryce Harper won the National League's 2015 Most Valuable Player (MVP) Award.

Billy Goat Curse

The 1945 World Series was memorable. The Chicago Cubs faced the Detroit Tigers. William Sianis was a Cubs fan. He tried to attend Game 4 at Wrigley Field. He brought his pet Billy goat along. But the goat wasn't allowed in the stadium.

Sianis grew angry. He **cursed** the Cubs.
He said they would never win another
World Series. The Cubs lost the 1945 World
Series. The Curse of the Billy Goat was born.

FACT

William's nephew, Sam Sianis, brought his goat to Wrigley Field several times. He hoped it might help end the Cubs' curse.

The curse lasted more than 70 years. The Cubs didn't win a World Series until 2016. That victory ended a **drought** of 108 years. Finally, the curse was broken!

Glossary

curse (KURS)—to wish for harm or misfortune to happen to someone

drought (DROUT)—a long period of time when a team does not win a championship

infield (IN-feeld)—the area of a baseball field that includes home plate and all three bases

influence (IN-floo-uhnss)—to have an effect on someone or something

inning (IN-ing)—a period of time in a baseball game when each team gets turns at bat until they get three outs

lore (LOHR)—the history and traditional knowledge or beliefs about something

myth (MITH)—a false idea that many people believe

predict (pri-DIKT)—to say what you think will happen in the future

umpire (UHM-pyr)—an official person who makes sure the game is played correctly and fairly

Read More

Berglund, Bruce. *Baseball GOATs: The Greatest Athletes of All Time*. North Mankato, MN: Capstone Press, 2022.

Smith, Elliott. *Football's Greatest Myths and Legends*. North Mankato, MN: Capstone Press, 2023.

Terrell, Brandon. *Calling His Shot: Babe Ruth's Legendary Home Run*. North Mankato, MN: Capstone Press, 2019.

Internet Sites

MLB Kids
mlb.com/fans/kids

MLB Play Ball
playball.org

Sports Illustrated Kids: Baseball
sikids.com/baseball

Index

About the Author

Elliott Smith is a former sports reporter who covered athletes in all sports from high school to the pros. He is one of the authors of the Natural Thrills series about extreme outdoor sports. In his spare time, he likes playing sports with his two children, going to the movies, and adding to his collection of Pittsburgh Steelers memorabilia.